Move with English

A Pupil's Book

Frances Bates–Treloar
Steve Thompson

Max   Bill   Sue   May   Pex   Sam

Marshall Cavendish
Education

Let's Start!

Move With English A has been developed to ensure that young learners build on the vocabulary and language skills acquired in Start With English. The **Pupil's Book** develops reading, listening and speaking skills for a wider range of contexts in line with the learner's own development. Learning is consolidated through each language skill, so that learners are always secure in their grasp of new vocabulary and language structures. The corresponding Workbook emphasises writing and provides focused practice and consolidation of the language items taught.

The Pupil's Book provides many opportunities for individual, pair and group work. Skills-focused activities help the learner use English fluently and confidently.

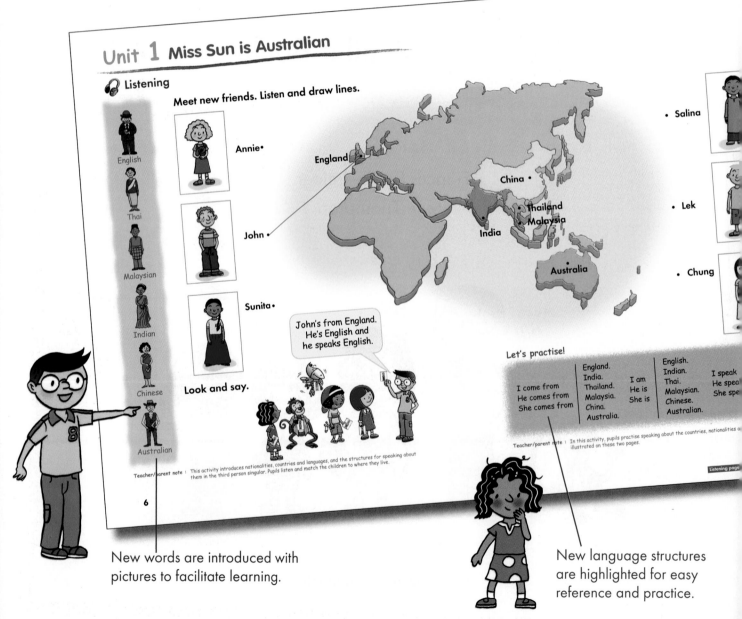

New words are introduced with pictures to facilitate learning.

New language structures are highlighted for easy reference and practice.

Language is presented and practised in lively situations. The songs, rhymes and games make learning enjoyable for young learners.

The teacher/parent note at the bottom of each page provides guidelines for meaningful parental involvement.

Cross-references point learners to activities in the Workbook for further practice on the items taught.

Revision units review and consolidate the vocabulary and structures taught. Activities are provided in assessment formats to develop the learner's confidence and facilitate the evaluation of outcomes.

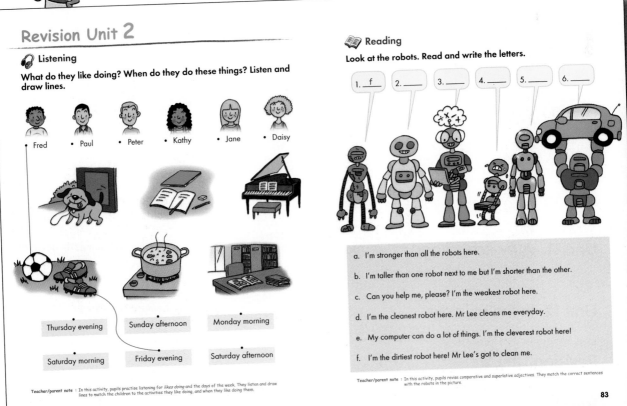

Contents

Structures	Functions
Simple present tense to introduce oneself Greetings Reinforcement of the meaning and use of *but*	Introducing oneself Using appropriate greetings at different times of the day
Reinforcement of *have got* and *is wearing* to describe physical appearances Reinforcement of the preposition *with* to describe physical appearances	Talking about physical appearances Asking and answering questions on how to identify people
Adverbs of frequency *always, often, sometimes* and *never* Reinforcement of simple present tense to express routines	Talking about animals and pets Asking and answering questions about daily routines
Modal verb *have (got) to* in present tense	Talking about what one and others have to do Asking and answering questions about what has to be done
Simple present tense to express general facts Reinforcement of interrogative pronouns *what, how, why, where* and *how many*	Talking about the weather Talking about pictures Asking and answering questions about pictures
Simple present tense to give directions Prepositions of location *above, below* and *opposite*	Giving directions Talking about the location of things Asking and answering questions about the location of things
Comparative adjectives	Talking about the differences between things and people
Superlative adjectives	Talking about the differences between things and people Talking about pictures Asking and answering questions about people and things
Days of the week Prepositions of location and time Reinforcement of interogative pronouns *how often* and *when*	Talking about schedules Asking and answering questions about schedules Talking about the frequency of activities Asking and answering questions about the frequency of activities
Modal verb *would like* to make requests	Talking about containers Making polite requests
The verb *like* to express likes and dislikes Adverbs of degree to express liking Reinforcement of adverbs of frequency	Talking about the degree of likes and dislikes Asking and answering questions about likes and dislikes
Reinforcement of prepositions Reinforcement of *and, but, so* and *because*	Asking and answering about people in a picture Asking and answering about food, leisure and routines

Unit 1 Miss Sun is Australian

🎧 Listening

Meet new friends. Listen and draw lines.

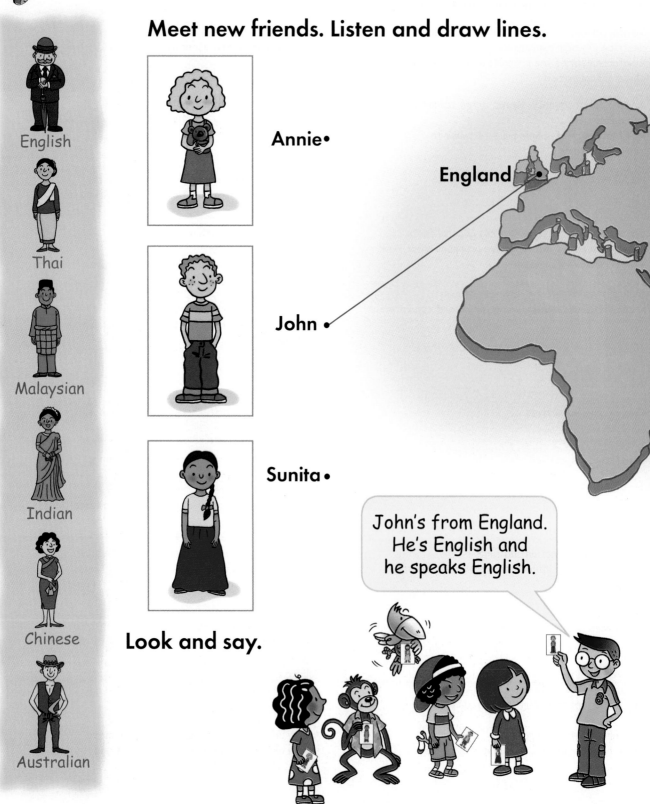

English

Thai

Malaysian

Indian

Chinese

Australian

Annie•

John •

Sunita •

England •

John's from England.
He's English and
he speaks English.

Look and say.

Teacher/parent note : This activity introduces nationalities, countries and languages, and the structures for speaking about them in the third person singular. Pupils listen and match the children to where they live.

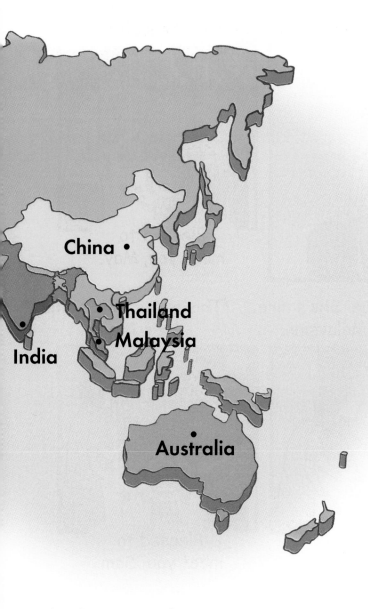

China •

• Thailand
• Malaysia

India

• Australia

• Salina

• Lek

• Chung

Let's practise!

I come from He comes from She comes from	England. India. Thailand. Malaysia. China. Australia.	I am He is She is	English. Indian. Thai. Malaysian. Chinese. Australian.	I speak He speaks She speaks	English. Hindi. Thai. Malay. Chinese. English.

Teacher/parent note : In this activity, pupils practise speaking about the countries, nationalities and languages of the children illustrated on these two pages.

📖 Reading

Read.

Good morning, everyone. This is Miss Sun. She's a new teacher at our school. She's from Australia.

This is May. She's eight. She's Chinese.

Pleased to meet you, May.

This is Bill. He's eight. He's Thai.

Pleased to meet you, Bill.

This is Sue. She's nine. She's Malaysian.

Pleased to meet you, Sue.

This is Sam. He's nine. He's Indian.

Pleased to meet you, Sam.

🎧 Listening

Listen and write the names.

1.    Miss Sun _____   2. _____

3. _____   4. _____

5. _____   6. _____

7. _____   8. _____

Teacher/parent note : This activity consolidates the use of nationalities, countries and languages in the context of introductions. Pupils read the text. They then listen to questions, and answer by writing the names of the characters.

Writing page 8 ▶

💬 Speaking

Introduce yourself.

Hello, I'm May. I'm eight. I'm from China.

Hello, May. Pleased to meet you.

Practise.

Hello, I'm Miss Sun. I'm Australian.

I'm sorry. I didn't hear you. What did you say?

I'm Miss Sun. I'm Australian.

Now introduce May, Bill, Sue and Sam to your friends.

This is Bill. He's eight. He's from Thailand.

Teacher/parent note : In the first activity, pupils practise introducing themselves and responding to instructions. In the second activity, they are introduced to more speech patterns. In the third activity, pupils practise introducing other pupils.

9

Speaking

coffee   a kangaroo

Listen and say.

Good morning, good morning,
the sun is coming up,
Good morning, good morning,
here's some coffee in a cup.

Good afternoon, good afternoon,
we are very hot,
Good afternoon, good afternoon,
we read and write a lot.

Good evening, good evening,
at home we talk and play,
Good evening, good evening,
we watch TV, hooray!

Good night, good night,
tired and sleepy heads,
Good night, good night,
we're going to our beds.

Teacher/parent note : In this activity, pupils learn greetings throughout the day. They listen and repeat the rhyme.

Writing page 10

Reading

Look at the pictures. Read and tick (✓).

Name: John
Age: 8 years old
Comes from: England
Speaks: English

Name: Annie
Age: 8 years old
Comes from: Australia
Speaks: English

Name: Chung
Age: 9 years old
Comes from: China
Speaks: Chinese

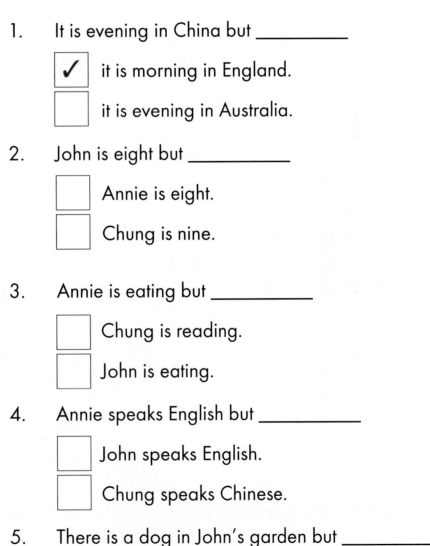

It is evening in China and it is evening in Australia.

It is evening in China but it is morning in England.

1. It is evening in China but _____

    ✓ it is morning in England.

    ☐ it is evening in Australia.

2. John is eight but _____

    ☐ Annie is eight.

    ☐ Chung is nine.

3. Annie is eating but _____

    ☐ Chung is reading.

    ☐ John is eating.

4. Annie speaks English but _____

    ☐ John speaks English.

    ☐ Chung speaks Chinese.

5. There is a dog in John's garden but _____

    ☐ there is a kangaroo in Annie's garden.

    ☐ there is a dog in Chung's garden.

Teacher/parent note : This activity consolidates the meaning and use of *but*. Pupils read about the children in the pictures and choose the appropriate ending for each sentence.

Unit 2 The pirates and the parrot

 curly hair   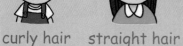 straight hair   blonde hair   a beard   a moustache   a shoulder   a neck

Listen and point.

Come and see
The Pirates and the Parrot

Teacher/parent note : This activity teaches vocabulary for describing physical appearance. Pupils listen to descriptive phrases
and point to the features of the pirates in the picture.

12

fair   quite tall   tall   very tall   fat   thin   a scarf   a coat

📖 Reading

Read and write the names.

He's got long hair. It's curly and blonde. He's got a moustache
and he's quite short. He is very fat.
He's called _____Jack_____.

This pirate's very short. He's got a long black beard,
but he hasn't got any hair! He's wearing a blue coat.
He's called _____.

He's got long curly black hair. He's tall and he isn't fair.
He's wearing a red scarf around his neck.
He's called _____.

He's got long straight hair. He's very thin and he's quite tall.
He's quite fair. He's got a parrot on his shoulder.
He's wearing a blue scarf around his neck.
He's called _____.

Teacher/parent note : In this activity, pupils practise reading the new vocabulary in context and revise the structures *have got* and *is wearing*. They read the text and write the names of the pirates described.

🎧 Listening

Listen and draw lines.

We're having a party!
What do you want to wear?

Bill

May

Sam

Sue

Teacher/parent note : This activity reinforces the new vocabulary in the context of dressing up as pirates. Pupils listen to the descriptions and match the characters with the things they want to wear.

Speaking page 14 ▶

Speaking

Look, point and say.

 He's got black hair and a black beard.

Talk about these people.

1. Yourself
2. Your friend
3. A man in your family
4. A woman in your family

Let's practise!

I have got (a) I've got (a)	curly straight	hair.
You have got (a) You've got (a)	blonde black brown	moustache.
He has got (a) He's got (a) She has got (a) She's got (a)	long short	beard.

Teacher/parent note : In the first activity, pupils use the new vocabulary to describe people in the pictures. In the second activity, they describe themselves and others.

📖 Reading

Look at the picture. Read and write yes or no.

1. The pirate with the black coat has got a parrot
    on his shoulder.   _____no_____

2. The pirate with the curly blonde hair is
    drinking lemonade.   _____

3. The pirate with the black beard is sitting in the tree. _____

4. The pirate with the black moustache has got a box.   _____

5. The pirate with the red scarf is looking at the monkey. _____

Teacher/parent note : In this activity, pupils read descriptive structures using *with* to identify people. They practise reading
the new vocabulary and then decide if the statements correctly describe the picture.

Listening page 16 ▶

 Speaking

Ask and answer. Use the words in the box to help you.

boat	watermelon	bag	hat
lemonade	ice-cream	kite	ball

 Who's got a ball?

The boy with the short curly black hair has got a ball.

Let's practise!

The pirate		black		is sitting.
The boy		brown	moustache	is drinking.
The man	with the	curly	beard	has got a parrot.
The girl		blonde	hair	has got a box.
The woman				

Teacher/parent note : This activity reinforces the use of *with* to describe people. Pupils talk about people in a picture and the objects they have got.

Unit 3 My friends, the animals

🎧 Listening

Look at the pictures. Listen and point. Then sing the song.

a lot   a bat

Do you know and can you say

the names of a lot of animals today?

Hippo, horse, kangaroo and bat.

Elephant, tiger, giraffe and cat.

Monkey, lizard, mouse and frog.

Cow and crocodile, goat and dog.

Now we know and we can say

The names of a lot of animals today.

Teacher/parent note : In this activity, pupils revise and expand their animal vocabulary using a song. They listen and point to the correct animals, then sing the song.

Writing page 18 ▶

Read and say.

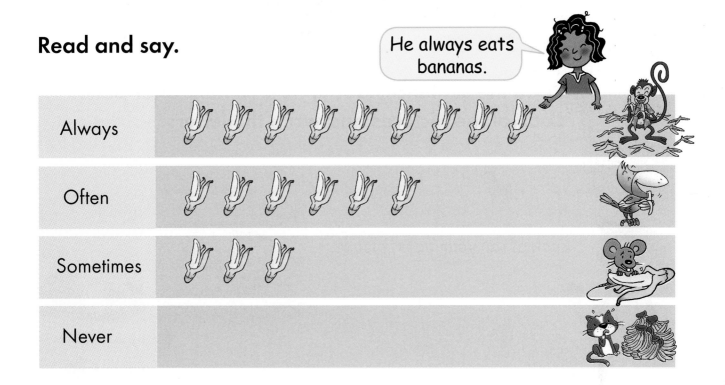

Listen and draw lines.

always   never   sometimes   often

Teacher/parent note : These activities familiarise pupils with the adverbs of frequency *often, always, never* and *sometimes*. Pupils listen to statements and identify the adverbs used.

Reading

a cage

Read the sentences about how to look after pets. Look at the pictures and write the letters.

Look after your pets, please.

A.

B.

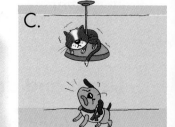
C.

1. Never leave your dog at home with a cat. _____C_____

2. Always say nice words to your dog. _____

3. Never leave your dog in a field with sheep. _____

4. Always close the door of your bird cage. _____

5. Always take your dog for a walk. _____

6. Never give your pet bird a lot of cake. _____

7. Always give your pet bird a lot of water. _____

8. Never leave your dog in a hot car. _____

9. Always give your dog the right food. _____

D.

E.

I.

H.

Good dog, Rover!

G.

F.

Teacher/parent note : This activity reinforces *always* and *never* in the context of instructions. Pupils read the sentences and match them with the correct pictures.

Writing page 20 ▶

Listen and read about Bill and his pets.

When I get up in the morning, I always go and see my pets. They are always awake before I get up. I say "hello" to Rover and Clover but I never play with them before school.

After school, I often play with my pet bird. It sometimes flies around my room and it sometimes sits on my shoulder.

In the afternoon, I always take Rover and Clover for a walk. Sometimes, we go to the park and sometimes we go to the playground.

At night, my bird always sleeps in my room. Rover and Clover never sleep in my room. They sleep in the garden.

Now read and tick (✓) or cross (✗).

1. Rover and Clover are always awake before Bill gets up.   ✓

2. Bill plays with Rover and Clover before school.   _____

3. Bill often plays with his pet bird after school.   _____

4. Bill always takes Rover and Clover for a walk.   _____

5. Bill, Rover and Clover always go to the park.   _____

6. Rover and Clover never sleep in Bill's room.   _____

Teacher/parent note : This activity lets pupils practise reading a text which contains adverbs of frequency. Pupils then read statements about the text and decide if they are true or false.

 Speaking

**How often do you do these? Write always, never, often
or sometimes.**

1.

Clean your pet's cage

_____

2.

Give water to an animal

_____

6.

Look after your pet

_____

7.

Draw pictures of your pet

_____

8.

Watch TV about animals

_____

**Talk about what you do with pets and animals. Let your friend
tell others about you.**

I often look after my pets.

Sam often looks after his pets.

Teacher/parent note : These activities allow pupils to speak about their own routines with pets. In the first activity, pupils
complete the illustrations with adverbs of frequency. In the second activity, they talk about how often
they do these things.

Take your pet for a walk

_____

4.

Give your pet a bath

_____

5.

Play with your pet

_____

9.

Give food to birds

_____

10.

Take photos of your pet

_____

Ask and answer.

 Do you look after your pets?

Oh yes! I always look after my pets. What about you?

Let's practise!

| always | often |
| sometimes | never |

Teacher/parent note : In this activity, pupils ask and answer questions using adverbs of frequency.

Unit 4 Helping at school and at home

📖 Reading

a bin   a brush   empty   rubbish   tidy   wash

Listen, read and say.

I've got to clean the board and I've got to tidy the books.

I've got to put the rubbish in the bin and I have to empty the bin.

I've got to wash the paint brushes and I have to tidy the pencils.

I've got to close the windows and I've got to put the chairs under the desks.

Now look at the pictures. Who has to do these things? Write the names.

Bill

Teacher/parent note : These activities teach the first person singular form of *have (got) to*. Pupils listen to and read sentences and then they match them with the correct pictures.

Listening page 24 ▶

Look at the picture. Tick (✓) the things they have done. Cross (✗) the things they have to do.

Things to do

1. We have to tidy the books.	✗
2. We have to put the rubbish into the bin.	_____
3. We've got to tidy the pencils.	_____
4. We have to close the windows.	_____
5. We've got to wash the paint brushes.	_____
6. We have to put the chairs under the desks.	_____
7. We've got to clean the board.	_____

Teacher/parent note : This activity teaches the first person plural form of *have (got) to*. Pupils read the list and identify the things the characters still have to do.

Listening

buy   a cup   a market   tea   wash up

Listen and write the numbers.

Say what the robot has to do and what he doesn't have to do.

 The robot has got to ...

The robot doesn't have to ...

Teacher/parent note : These activities teach the negative form of *have (got) to*. In the first activity, pupils listen and number the pictures according to the information given. The second activity teaches the negative form of *have (got) to* in the third person singular.

Speaking page 26 ▶

Speaking

Listen, point and say.

I have to be good in school.

I don't have to take tests.

I sometimes have to sleep in the garden.

I don't have to talk to people.

What do you have to do? Tick (✓) or cross (✗).

- [ ] Help in the garden.
- [ ] Clean the bedroom.
- [ ] Empty the rubbish bin.
- [ ] Clean the kitchen.
- [ ] Tidy the clothes.

- [ ] Wash up.
- [ ] Tidy the sitting room.
- [ ] Wash the floor.
- [ ] Cook dinner.
- [ ] Buy food at the market.

Now ask and answer.

What do you have to do at home?

I have to ...

Teacher/parent note : In the first activity, pupils listen and say sentences. In the second and third activities, pupils practise talking about what they have or don't have to do to help at home.

Listening

Who is going to the party? Listen and tick (✓) or cross (✗).

Can you come to my birthday party?

| May ✓ | Sam | Bill | Sue |

What do they have to do? Now listen again and draw lines.

Teacher/parent note : These activities consolidate pupils' understanding of *have (got) to*. They listen to four short conversations and decide which characters can go to the party. They then identify the tasks each character has to do.

Reading page 28

 ## Speaking

Ask and answer. What do they have to do before Jill's party?

What has May got to do before the party?

She's got to clean her bedroom and she's got to ...

Ask and answer. What do you have to do to help out at home and at school? What don't you have to do?

Have you got to help out at home?

Yes, I have to tidy the books but I don't have to empty the bins.

Say three things your friend has to do to help out.

May's got to wash up. She's got to ...

Let's practise!

I We You	have (got) to ... don't have to ...	Have you	
			got to ...?
She He	has (got) to ... doesn't have to ...	Has she he	

Teacher/parent note : These activities let pupils ask questions using *have (got) to*. In pairs, they talk about what the characters have to do. They then use these structures to exchange information about themselves. Finally, they talk about what their friends have to do.

Writing page 29

Unit 5 The weather's very nice

🎧 Listening

blow   hot   shine   snow   wet   windy

Listen and point.

1.   2.

3.   4.

Listen and write the numbers.

Teacher/parent note : These activities introduce weather vocabulary. First, pupils listen to and repeat dialogues presenting weather vocabulary. They then listen to short descriptive sentences and number the pictures.

 cold  weather  cloudy  rain

Listen, read and draw lines. Then sing the song.

The weather's very hot today.
The sky is blue. What can we do?
The sun is shining. It's hot today.
We want to play this morning.

The weather's very cold today.
There's a lot of ice. It's very nice.
It's snowing and it's cold today.
We want to play this morning.

The weather's very wet today.
The sky is grey. Can we play?
It's raining and it's wet today.
We want to play this morning.

The weather's very nice today.
It's a cloudy sky. Can we fly?
The wind is blowing. It's a windy day.
We want to play this morning.

Teacher/parent note : These activities teach more weather vocabulary and consolidate pupils' ability to understand details in sentences. First, pupils listen, read and match the verses of the song with the appropriate pictures. They then sing the song.

 **Reading**

Bill is reading about a holiday in a forest.

Listen and read.

a forest

a holiday

a mountain

a river

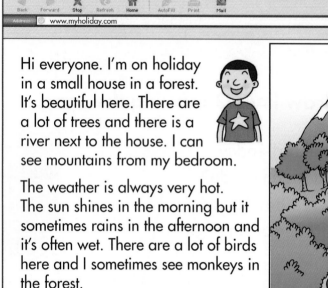

www.myholiday.com

Hi everyone. I'm on holiday in a small house in a forest. It's beautiful here. There are a lot of trees and there is a river next to the house. I can see mountains from my bedroom.

The weather is always very hot. The sun shines in the morning but it sometimes rains in the afternoon and it's often wet. There are a lot of birds here and I sometimes see monkeys in the forest.

Jim, 10 years old

Read and tick (✓) or cross (✗).

1. Jim is 10 years old.   ✓ _____

2. He's on holiday in the mountains.   _____

3. He's in a big house.   _____

4. Jim can see a river from his bedroom.   _____

5. The house is next to the river.   _____

6. The weather is always very hot.   _____

7. The sun always shines in the afternoon.   _____

8. Jim sometimes sees monkeys in the forest. _____

Teacher/parent note : In this activity, pupils read and comprehend a short text. They then read statements about the text and decide if they are true or false.

Listening page 32

Listen and read.

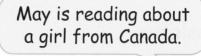
May is reading about a girl from Canada.

a whale

Canada

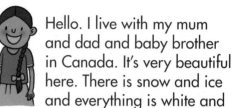

Address: www.whereilive.com

Hello. I live with my mum and dad and baby brother in Canada. It's very beautiful here. There is snow and ice and everything is white and clean. The weather is very cold and windy and it often snows. The days are short and the nights are very long.

The sea water is very cold here but there are a lot of fish in the sea. I sometimes see whales here. There are a lot of birds too.

Jane, 8 years old

Read and circle the answers.

1. How old is Jane?   (a) 8 years old)   b) 10 years old

2. How many people live with Jane?   a) Three   b) Four

3. Where does Jane live?   a) A hot place   b) A cold place

4. Why is everything white?   a) It often snows. b) The wind often blows.

5. What is in the sea?   a) A lot of birds   b) A lot of fish

6. What can Jane sometimes see?   a) Birds   b) Whales

7. What are the days like?   a) Short   b) Very long

Teacher/parent note : In this activity, pupils read another short text. They revise *wh-* questions and choose the best answers to the questions.

Speaking

Look at the pictures. Talk about them.

a sweater

Sue is wearing a red scarf.

A   Sue

B   Bill   Sam

C   Mary   Sue

D   Mr Lee   Robot

Teacher/parent note : In this activity, pupils look at the pictures and talk about them.

Now ask and answer.

How many people are there?
What are they wearing?
What are they doing?
What else is happening?
What else can you see?
Is the weather nice? Why? Why not?

What is Sue wearing in Picture A?

She's wearing a red scarf, a yellow sweater and green trousers.

Say some true and some false sentences about each picture. Let your friend correct you.

There are two people in picture A.

No, that's not true. There is ...

Let your friend choose a picture. Ask three questions about it. Can you guess which picture it is?

Is there a girl in this picture?

No, there isn't.

Is there a river in this picture?

Yes, there is.

Teacher/parent note : In the first activity, pupils consolidate new and previously taught vocabulary and structures and develop their ability to talk about pictures. In the second activity, pupils revise negative and affirmative forms. In the third activity, they practise using interrogative forms.

35

Unit **6** New places to live

 Listening

first   second   third   fourth   fifth   sixth   seventh

Max and Pex are going to visit their friends. Listen, point and say.

Walk past the first house
and past the second shop.
Walk to the third tree.
Stop! That's where I live.

Walk past the fourth cat.
Don't stop for the fifth mouse.
I live in the sixth nest
in the tree next to the seventh house.

Teacher/parent note : This activity introduces the ordinal numbers *first* through *tenth*. Pupils listen to a rhyme containing simple directions.

36

eighth

ninth

tenth

a nest

a shop

Fly into the eighth garden.
That's where you can find me.
That's where the ninth nest is,
up in the tenth tall tree.

Look at the picture again. Ask and answer.

Where's the pink bird's nest?

It's in the fourth garden.

Teacher/parent note : In this activity, pupils consolidate ordinal numbers and practise giving simple directions.

📖 Reading

a bank

a bus station

a café

a cinema

a hospital

a library

Read. Then number the places.

Hi Molly,

Are you OK? I've got some photos for you.
The first photo is of my new house. The second is of
the library. The next photo shows the supermarket.
I go shopping at the supermarket every Friday.
The fourth photo shows the cinema and the next
one shows the hospital. The sixth picture is of my
favourite café and the seventh picture is of the
swimming pool. I swim there every week. The eighth
picture shows the bank and the last picture is of
the bus station. Why have I got a picture of the bus
station? I take the bus from there to school.
That's why!

Bye!
Sue

Teacher/parent note : This activity reinforces ordinal numbers and introduces vocabulary connected with local places.

38

Speaking

 a swimming pool  a supermarket  above  below  opposite

Listen and say. Then ask and answer.

 Where's the cat in the first picture?

It's in front of the box.

Say where these places are.

Sue's house is on Market Street, opposite the hospital.

Teacher/parent note : In the first activity, pupils revise and extend their knowledge of prepositions of location. The second activity consolidates these prepositions. Pupils look at a map and describe where local places are.

Listening

a basement   ground floor   a lift

Look at the building. Listen and write the numbers.

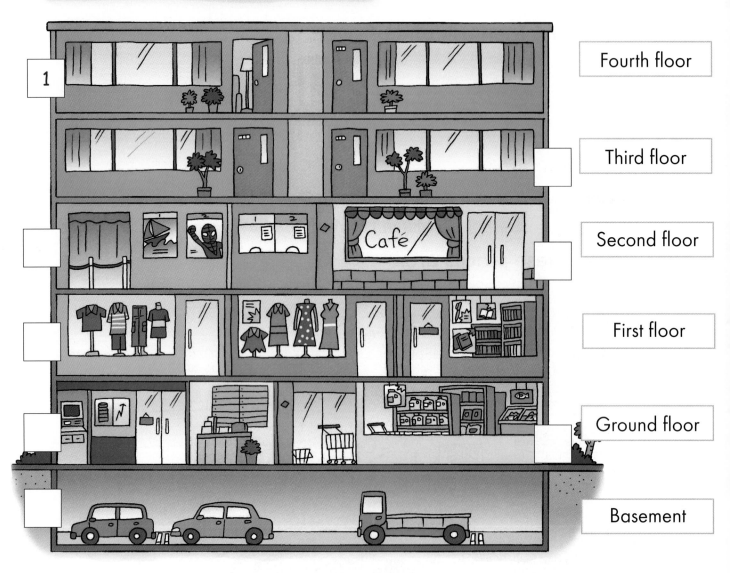

1

Fourth floor

Third floor

Second floor

First floor

Ground floor

Basement

Where do you want to go?

I want to go to the cafè.

Teacher/parent note : This activity consolidates vocabulary introduced in this unit. Pupils practise understanding dialogues containing simple directions.

Reading

Read Sue's letter. Ask and answer.

Hi again Molly,

Here's another picture for you. My friend, Peter, lives in this big building near my house. Peter's family lives in Flat 4A. It's on the fourth floor, so Peter always takes the lift to his flat!

Sue

1. Who lives in this building?
2. Where is the building?
3. Does Peter's family live in a house?
4. What is the number of Peter's flat?
5. Why does Peter take the lift?

Who lives in this building?

Sue's friend, Peter, lives in this building.

Look at the picture on page 40. Read and tick (✓) or cross (✗).

1. Peter's family lives in this building. _____✓_____
2. There are seven floors in Peter's building. _____
3. The clothes shops are next to the library. _____
4. There are four cars in the picture. _____
5. The cars are on the ground floor. _____
6. The cinema is on the second floor. _____
7. Peter's flat is on the third floor. _____
8. There are two flats on the fourth floor. _____

Teacher/parent note : These activities introduce vocabulary to describe parts of a building. In the first activity, pupils answer questions about a short e-mail. In the second activity, they decide if statements about the building are true or false.

Revision Unit 1

🎧 Listening

What have they got to do? Listen and draw lines.

• Fred   • Paul   • Peter   • Kathy   • Jane   • Daisy

Teacher/parent note : In this activity, pupils practise the structure *have got to* and vocabulary related to chores. They then match the children's names to the chores they have to do.

42

 **Reading**

Look at the children on page 42. Read and write their names.

I am quite tall. I have got short straight blonde hair. My name is ___Peter___.

I have got long curly black hair. I am short. My name is _____.

I have got long straight blonde hair. I am quite tall. My name is _____.

I am very tall and I have got short straight black hair. My name is _____.

I have got short curly black hair. I am quite short. My name is _____.

I am very tall. I have got short curly blonde hair. My name is _____.

Read and draw.

I am a man. I have got short curly brown hair. I have got a brown moustache and a brown beard. I am wearing a blue T-shirt and black trousers.

Teacher/parent note : The first activity revises descriptions of physical appearance. Pupils read the short texts and write the names of the children described. In the second activity, pupils draw and colour a man according to a descriptive text.

Speaking

Look at the pictures and talk about the weather in your country. Use the words in the box to help you.

In my country, it's often hot.

It sometimes rains in my country.

| never | sometimes | often | always |

Ask and answer.

Is it raining or is the sun shining today?

The sun is shining.

Is the weather hot or cold now?

It's cold.

What colour is the sky?

The sky is blue today.

Teacher/parent note : In the first activity, pupils revise adverbs of frequency and weather vocabulary. They then ask and answer questions about the weather today.

 Reading

What are these places? Read and write the words.

1. It is very big. Often there is snow on top of it.   a mountain

2. You can eat and drink here.   _____

3. There are a lot of trees here.   _____

4. You can catch a bus here.   _____

5. You buy fruits and vegetables here.   _____

6. Fish live in it. Sometimes it is very long.   _____

7. You have lessons here.   _____

8. You buy fruit, bread and meat here.   _____

Teacher/parent note : This activity revises vocabulary related to local places and geographical features. Pupils read the clues and write what is being described.

Speaking

The children are helping Mr Lee make a robot. Listen and point.

a square

round

afraid

strong

tired

a wheel

Max

Bill

Sue

Teacher/parent note : These activities introduce some new adjectives and revise previously taught adjectives. Pupils use the words to make sentences about the picture.

Pex

May

Mr Square

Mr Lee

Sam

strong

dirty

tired

clean

wet

square

big

afraid

small

happy

round

Point and say. Use the words in the box to help you.

Sue is dirty.

Reading

Read and tick (✓) the correct answers.

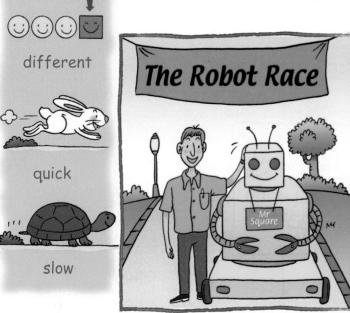

different

quick

slow

Today, there is a robot race in the park. Mr Lee is in the park with Mr Square.

1. Where is the robot race?

  ✓ In the park

  ☐ At school

  ☐ At the shops

2. Who is with Mr Lee?

  ☐ A man

  ☐ A teacher

  ☐ A robot

There are three robots in the race.
They are all different.

3. Which robot is smaller than Mr Square?

  ☐ Animal

  ☐ Big Ben

4. Which robot is bigger than Mr Square?

  ☐ Animal

  ☐ Big Ben

Teacher/parent note : The activity on these two pages introduces comparative adjectives in the context of a story. Pupils read the text and answer questions about it.

Look at the robots! Two are quick but one is slow.

5. Which robot is quicker than Big Ben?

☐ Animal

☐ Mr Square

6. Which robot is slower than Big Ben?

☐ Animal

☐ Mr Square

The race is over. Mr Square is first! Mr Lee is very happy.

7. Who is second?

☐ Mr Lee

☐ Big Ben

☐ Animal

8. Why is Mr Lee happy?

☐ Animal is slower than Big Ben.

☐ The race is over.

☐ Mr Square is quicker than

Animal and Big Ben.

Listening

Listen and repeat.

loud

taller	shorter	bigger
stronger	louder	better
dirtier	more beautiful	more afraid

Now listen and tick (✓).

1.

✓ ☐

2.

☐ ☐

3.

☐ ☐

4.

☐ ☐

5.

☐ ☐

6.

☐ ☐

Teacher/parent note : The first activity reinforces *-er* and *more ...* as structures for forming comparative adjectives. In the second activity, pupils listen to statements with comparative adjectives and tick the pictures that illustrate them.

7.

8.

9.

10.

Let's practise!

| ... is | taller

dirtier

better
worse

more beautiful | than ... |

Unit 8 Welcome to Coco Island!

Speaking

an island

Mr Lee and the children are going to Coco Island. Listen, look and say.

the biggest lake	the highest mountain	the longest river
the biggest forest	the longest beach	the shortest beach
the oldest building	the smallest town	the best café

This is Great Lake. Great Lake is the biggest lake on Coco Island.

Teacher/parent note : In this activity, pupils say sentences using superlative adjectives. They look at the map and role-play the island guide, describing the features on the island.

Writing page 52 ➤

 **Reading**

Look at the map again. Read and write.

1. Which is the shortest river? _____Slow River_____

2. Which is the smallest forest? _____

3. Which is the highest mountain? _____

4. Which is the smallest lake? _____

5. Which is the longest beach? _____

6. Which is the biggest town? _____

Teacher/parent note : In this activity, pupils read questions using superlative adjectives and write the answers.

📖 Reading

Read and write the words.

small	smaller than	the smallest
long	longer than	the longest
short	shorter than	the shortest
high	higher than	the highest
quiet	quieter than	1. _____
big	bi**gg**er than	the bi**gg**est
fat	fa**tt**er than	2. _____
silly	sill**i**er than	the sill**i**est
noisy	nois**i**er than	3. _____
angry	angr**i**er than	the angr**i**est
beautiful	**more** beautiful than	the **most** beautiful
afraid	**more** afraid than	4. _____
good	**better** than	the **best**
bad	**worse** than	the **worst**

Tick (✓) the correct pictures.

1. The smallest animal

 ✓    ☐    ☐

2. The longest scarf

 ☐    ☐   ☐

3. The tallest building

 ☐   ☐   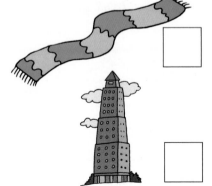 ☐

Teacher/parent note : In the first activity, pupils work out patterns for irregular superlative adjectives. In the second activity, they read phrases with superlative adjectives and tick the correct pictures.

Listening page 54 ▶

 **Listening**

Look at the pictures. Listen and write A to F.

You can find these animals on Coco Island.

1. _____F_____   2. _____   3. _____

4. _____   5. _____   6. _____

Teacher/parent note : In this activity, pupils practise listening to questions using superlative adjectives and *Which* ...? They then answer them by writing the appropriate letters.

🎧 Listening

Listen and write the numbers.

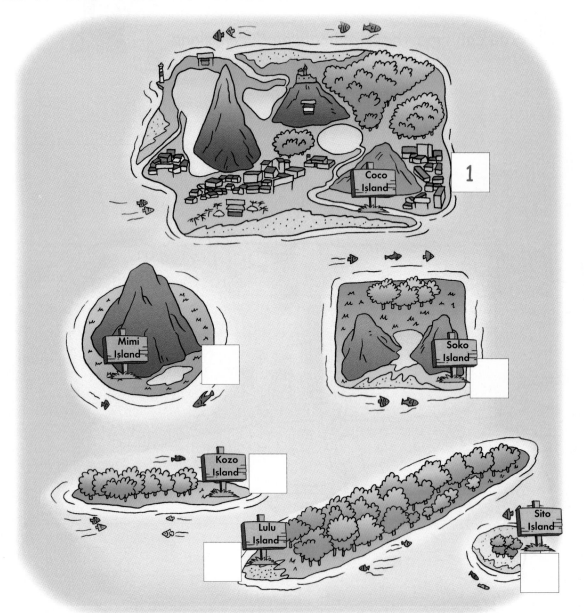

Where do they want to go? Listen, look at the picture and write.

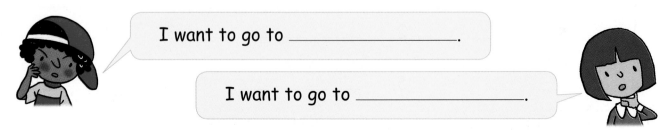

I want to go to _____.

I want to go to _____.

Teacher/parent note : In the first activity, pupils listen to statements using superlatives and number the islands described according to the statements they hear. In the second activity, pupils listen to descriptions and identify the islands described.

Speaking page 56 ▶

💬 Speaking

Ask and answer. Use the words in the boxes to help you.

Who is the tallest in the picture?

Mr Lee is the tallest.

Who is ...

the tallest?
the strongest child?
the saddest?
the shortest?
the oldest?

Who is ...

the fastest?
the slowest?
the hottest?
the angriest?

Who is ...

the hungriest?
the happiest?
the most tired?
the most afraid?

Teacher/parent note : In this activity, pupils practise using superlatives to ask and answer questions about the pictures, as prompted by the words provided.

Unit 9 Can you come to the party?

🎧 **Listening**

Listen and tick (✓) or cross (✗).

	May	Bill	Sam
Monday	✓	☐	☐
Tuesday	✗	☐	☐
Wednesday	✗	☐	☐
Thursday	✓	☐	☐
Friday	✗	☐	☐
Saturday	✗	☐	☐
Sunday	✓	☐	☐

When can everyone go to Sue's party?

On _____.

Teacher/parent note : This activity introduces pupils to the days of the week. Pupils listen and understand the gist of the dialogues to find out when everyone can attend Sue's party.

Writing page 58 ➤

Listen again. What does Bill have to do? Draw lines.

Monday

Tuesday

Wednesday

Thursday

Friday

Saturday

Sunday

Teacher/parent note : In this activity, pupils practise listening for specific information concerning the days of the week to find out what Bill does on each day of the week.

Speaking

homework   visit

You want to go to the park with your friend. Find a time. Ask and answer.

Diary 1

Saturday		Sunday	
Morning	: free	Morning	: visit my grandparents
Afternoon	: free	Afternoon	: free
Evening	: do my homework	Evening	: free

Can you come to the park on Saturday morning?

No, I can't. I help Mum and Dad at home on Saturday mornings.

Diary 2

Saturday		Sunday	
Morning	:help Mum and Dad at home	Morning	:go for a walk with my family
Afternoon	:swimming lessons	Afternoon	:free
Evening	:free	Evening	:do my homework

When can you go to the park?

On _____.

Teacher/parent note : This activity teaches pupils the structures for asking and answering questions about schedules. In pairs, pupils use the diary pages to role-play and find out when they are both free.

Reading pages 60 – 61 ▶

 **Reading**

Read. Write your name.

Dear _____,

Come to my party!

My birthday party is on
Sunday afternoon
at
the beach (for games)

and then at
my house (for cake)

Can you come? Tell me before
Wednesday.

From,
Sue

Now write the words.

after	at	at	before	in	on	to	to

Sue wants you to go _____to_____ her party! The party is _____

Sunday _____ the afternoon. It is _____ the beach. _____

the games at the beach, there is a birthday tea _____ Sue's house.

You have to answer the invitation _____ Wednesday.

Teacher/parent note : This activity gives pupils practice using prepositions. They read the invitation, then complete the blanks in a short text about it.

Reading

Read and tick (✓) the answers.

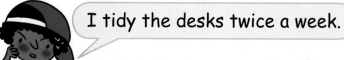
I tidy the desks twice a week.

	Monday	Tuesday	Wednesday	Thursday	Friday
Tidy the desks	Sam	Sue	Bill	May	Sam
Tidy the cupboards	Sue	Bill	May	Sam	Sue
Clean the floor	Bill	May	Sam	Sue	Bill
Empty the bins	May	Sam	Sue	Bill	May
Close the windows	Mr Lee	Mr Lee	Mr Lee	Mr Lee	Mr Lee
Look after the class mouse	Sam	Sue	Bill	May	Mr Lee

1. How often does Sam have to tidy the desks?

   [✓] twice a week   [ ] on Mondays   [ ] every day

2. When does Sue have to clean the floor?

   [ ] twice a week   [ ] on Thursdays   [ ] every day

   I tidy the cupboards once a week.

3. When does May have to empty the bins?

   [ ] every Tuesday   [ ] never   [ ] on Mondays and Fridays

4. How often does Mr Lee have to close the windows?

   [ ] every day   [ ] twice a week   [ ] once a week

5. When does Bill have to look after the class mouse?

   [ ] on Mondays   [ ] on Tuesdays   [ ] on Wednesdays

Teacher/parent note : This activity teaches the structures *How often ...?* and *When ...?* to ask questions about frequency and the days of the week. They read the rota and answer questions about it.

Writing page 62 ▶

Speaking

soup

Look at the pictures. Ask and answer.

fish	soup	sausages
eggs	chicken	ice-cream

on Mondays

on Tuesdays

on Wednesdays

on Thursdays

on Fridays

on Saturdays

on Sundays

How often does Mr Lee have sausages for lunch?

He has sausages twice a week.

When does Mr Lee have sausages for lunch?

He has sausages on Mondays and Thursdays.

Let's practise!

How often does ...?	once a week
	twice a week
When does ...?	on Mondays

Teacher/parent note : In this activity, pupils practise using the structures *How often ...?* and *When ...?* to ask questions about frequency and the days of the week.

63

Unit 10 The picnic by the waterfall

a bowl

a bottle

a plate

a sandwich

a picnic

a waterfall

 Reading

Look at Picture 1. Read and strike out the wrong words.

1. There are two ~~cups~~ / bowls of fruit.

2. There are some bottles / glasses of lemonade.

3. There is a bag / box of toys.

4. There are some bags / boxes of clothes.

5. There is a cup / bottle of water.

6. There are some bowls / plates of sandwiches.

Look at the pictures on pages 64 — 65. Read and write the letters.

a. Bill and Sam are drinking glasses of orange juice.

b. Max is wearing a blue bowl!

c. Now Pex has got nothing in his bowl!

d. Bill and Sam have got a plate of sandwiches.

e. Pex and Max are having a picnic by the waterfall too. They haven't got any food.

f. Bill, Sam and Bill's parents are having a picnic by the waterfall.

g. Pex and Max have got bowls of fruit.

h. Pex isn't looking at his bowl of fruit.

Teacher/parent note : These activities introduce pupils to vocabulary relating to containers. Pupils look at the pictures and strike out the wrong words. They then match the sentences in the box with the correct pictures on pages 64 — 65.

Listening page 64 ▶

Let's practise!

a bowl of	fruit
a cup of	water
a bottle of	juice
a plate of	sandwiches

Listening

Listen and number the pictures 1 to 7.

Teacher/parent note : This activity consolidates vocabulary relating to containers. Pupils listen and number the items according to the information provided.

Speaking page 66 – 67

 **Speaking**

Look at the pictures on page 66. Choose and draw five things on the shelf.

What is on your friend's shelf? Ask and answer. Tick (✓) the things.

 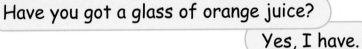 

Have you got a bottle of orange juice?

No, I haven't.

Have you got a glass of orange juice?

Yes, I have.

☐	a bottle of milk	☐	a bag of apples
☐	a glass of milk	☐	a bowl of apples
☐	a bottle of orange juice	☐	a cup of soup
☐	a glass of orange juice	☐	a bowl of soup
☐	a box of bananas	☐	a plate of cakes
☐	a bowl of bananas	☐	a box of cakes
☐	a bowl of rice	☐	a plate of rice

Teacher/parent note : This activity lets pupils practise saying the new vocabulary. They draw five items from page 66, then work in pairs to find out what their partners have drawn.

Listening

Listen and repeat.

Listen again. Draw lines.

Teacher/parent note : These activities introduce pupils to *would like* as a polite request. Pupils listen and repeat the dialogue. They then draw lines to match the speech bubbles with the speakers.

Writing page 68 ➤

Speaking

menu

Look at the menu. Ask and answer.

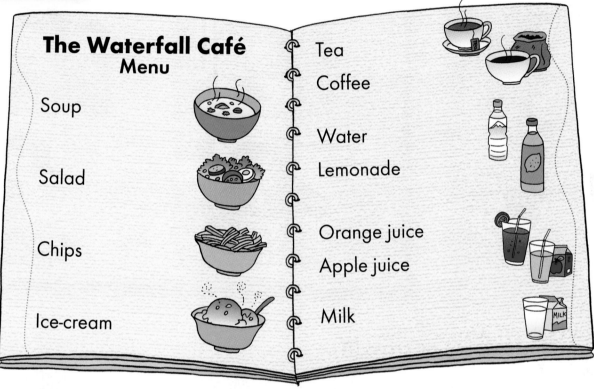

The Waterfall Café
Menu

Soup

Salad

Chips

Ice-cream

Tea

Coffee

Water

Lemonade

Orange juice

Apple juice

Milk

Which drink would you like?

I'd like a glass of orange juice, please.

What would you like?

I'd like a bowl of soup, please.

Let's practise!

What would you like?	I would like ... I'd like ...

Teacher/parent note : This activity gives pupils further practice asking and answering questions with *would like*. Pupils work in pairs or groups to ask for items from the café menu.

Unit 11 After school and at weekends

skating

sailing

weekend

shopping

Listening

Look at the pictures on pages 70 – 71. Listen, point and say.

1.

2.

6.

7.

Listen and tick (✓) or cross (✗).

	Sam	May	Sue	Bill
Shopping				
Doing homework				
Emptying bins				
Playing tennis				
Skating				
Drawing				
Sailing	✓			
Fishing				
Washing up				

Teacher/parent note : The first activity revises and extends vocabulary related to leisure and domestic activities. In the second activity, pupils listen to dialogues and identify what the characters like and don't like doing.

Writing page 70

💬 Speaking

Say what they like doing. Say what they don't like doing.

> Sam likes fishing but he doesn't like washing up.

Now say what you like doing. Say what you don't like doing.

> I like shopping but I don't like playing tennis.

Teacher/parent note : These activities give pupils practice using *like* with verbs in the infinitive form. First, they practise saying what the characters like and don't like doing. They then say what they like and don't like doing.

Reading

Read. Ask and answer.

invent

make

The Robot-maker

Mr Lee is a teacher. He has a very unusual hobby. He makes robots. "I enjoy inventing and making robots at the weekends. Sometimes, it is quite difficult to find all the things I need. There is always something wrong with my old robots so I make new ones. These are my four newest robots.

"I like the first robot. He is clever. He can sing and write but he isn't very fast. The second robot isn't very good. He isn't very strong but I like him. He's always happy. The third robot is strong but I don't like him. He's slow and silly and he has got a sad face. He likes to hide in the bathroom. I like the fourth robot best. He isn't fast but he's very nice. He always brings me a cup of tea in bed in the morning."

Who has got an unusual hobby?
What does he enjoy doing at the weekends?
How many robots are there in the picture?
Which robot does he like the best?

Who has got an unusual hobby?

Mr Lee has got an unusual hobby.

Read and strike out the wrong words.

1. Mr Lee is a ~~robot~~ / teacher .

2. Mr Lee makes robots after school / at the weekends .

3. The first robot is / isn't very fast.

4. The second robot is / isn't happy.

5. Mr Lee doesn't like / likes the second robot.

6. The third robot has got a slow / sad face.

7. The fourth robot is fast / slow but nice.

Teacher/parent note : These activities teach adverbs of degree to express liking. Pupils read a magazine article, and ask and answer questions about it. They then consolidate their understanding by reading statements about the article and striking out the wrong words.

Listening page 72 ▶

Read. Write the numbers.

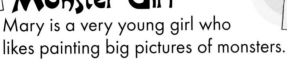

Monster Girl

Mary is a very young girl who likes painting big pictures of monsters.

"I enjoy drawing and painting monsters. I like painting my monsters at the weekends. My sister Sue sometimes helps me after school. These are six of my pictures.

"My first monster has got six legs. I like him a lot.
My second monster has got a moustache and a beard.
I don't like him. I don't like my third monster too. He's got long ears and he's nice. Nobody is afraid of him. I like my fourth picture the best. I like the monster's square eyes and round face. I quite like my fifth picture. I like the monster's green face and blue eyes. I like the sixth monster a lot. He's got a silly face and a strong body. The cat's afraid of him."

1

Now, talk about the pictures. How much does Mary like the monsters? How much do you like the monsters?

Mary likes the first monster a lot. It's got six legs.

Teacher/parent note : These activities give further practise on using adverbs of degree to express liking. Pupils read the magazine article and number the pictures according to the descriptions. They then talk about the pictures.

Listening

What do Ogg and Egg have to do? Listen and write the numbers.

hate

Ogg   Egg

1

Teacher/parent note : This activity reinforces the contrast of infinitive forms following the verbs *have* and *like*. Pupils listen and identify what the monsters have to do.

Writing page 74

How much do they like doing these things? Listen and draw lines.

Ogg

going to the pet shop	likes ... the best
cooking supper	likes ... a lot
eating a picnic in a tree	quite likes
washing the car	doesn't like
taking the dog for a walk	hates

Egg

- going shopping
- feeding the pet bird
- doing his homework
- bathing the pet lizard
- emptying the rubbish bin

💬 Speaking

Say what Ogg and Egg have to do.

Ogg has to go to the pet shop at weekends.

Say how much Ogg and Egg like doing these things.

Ogg likes going to the pet shop the best.

Do you like doing these things? Ask and answer.

Do you like washing the car?

Yes, I do. I quite like washing the car.

No, I don't. I don't like washing the car.

Let's practise!

likes ... the best   likes ... a lot   quite likes   doesn't like   hates

Teacher/parent note : In the first activity, pupils listen to find out how much Ogg and Egg enjoy what they have to do. In the second and third activities, pupils say what the monsters have to do and how much they like doing them. Pupils then talk about how much they like doing these things.

Unit 12 In the holidays

 Reading

a village

a farm

bottom

a letter

Read. Write the names.

It's a letter from Molly!

Dear Sue,

Hi! I'm on holiday with pupils and teachers from my school. We're in a beautiful English village. It's different from Liverpool, the city I live in. The village is near a farm. We visit it every day. There's a lake and we can swim and sail in it. We can also climb mountains and walk in the forest.

There's a school at the bottom of the mountain. We're visiting the school in the afternoon. The pupils and teachers there are very nice. Here is a photo of my new friends. Can you guess who's who?

Love,
Molly

Miss Rivers

_____

_____

Can you guess **who's who?**

1. Ryan has got curly black hair.
2. Miss Rivers is wearing a coat.
3. Gwen is wearing a green skirt.
4. Mr Adams isn't the tallest person.
5. Kelly is wearing green trousers.
6. Dave is taller than Rob.

Teacher/parent note : These activities revise vocabulary relating to physical appearances and geography. Pupils read a description to identify the people in a picture.

 **Speaking**

Now ask and answer.

Who is Molly writing to?   Who is Molly with?

Where is Molly?   What sports can Molly play there?

What else can Molly do there?   Who are Molly's new friends?

Look at the picture. Say where each person is standing. Use the words in the box to help you.

next to   between

Kelly is standing between Rob and Ryan.

Say what they are wearing.

Miss Rivers is wearing a brown coat, a green sweater and black trousers.

Teacher/parent note : In the first activity, pupils read the letter on page 76 again and ask and answer questions about it.
The second activity revises prepositions. The third activity revises *and* as well as articles of clothing.

Listening

Listen and tick (✓) or cross (✗).

1. Molly is talking to her mother. ____✓____

2. It's Molly's third week on holiday. _____

3. Molly is having a good time. _____

4. The weather in Liverpool is wet. _____

5. Molly's got English lessons in
   the morning. _____

Now complete these sentences using but.

1. Molly's got a sweater and a coat ...
2. It's wet in Liverpool ...
3. Molly's got an English lesson ...

Molly has got a sweater and a coat ...

... but it isn't cold so she doesn't have to wear them.

Listen and write the words.

	Morning	Afternoon	Evening
Monday	English	swimming	_____
Tuesday	English	_____	_____
Wednesday	_____	_____	singing
Thursday	_____	walking	_____
Friday	_____	_____	free

Teacher/parent note : These activities consolidate *but* and revise vocabulary related to food, leisure and routines. Pupils listen to a conversation and decide if statements about it are true or false. They then complete sentences using *but*. They listen to a further conversation and complete Molly's timetable.

Reading page 78

💬 Speaking

It's holiday time! Do you do these things? Tick (✓) or cross (✗). Then ask and answer.

	You	Your friend
Get up early		
Eat a big breakfast		
Do homework		
Go to the beach		
Read a book		
Play in the park		
Clean your room		
Visit your friends		
Go for a walk		

Do you get up early on holidays?

No, I don't.

Are holidays different from school days? Use the words in the boxes to help you.

and	but

always	never	sometimes	often

I never get up early on holidays but I always get up early on school days.

I sometimes eat a big breakfast on holidays and I sometimes eat a big breakfast on school days.

Teacher/parent note : These activities consolidate *and* and *but*. Pupils ask and answer about holiday routines. They then compare and contrast these with their routines on school days, joining their sentences with *and* or *but*.

 # Listening

Who wants to go for a walk? Listen and write the names.

Dave	Gwen	Kelly	Molly	Ryan	Rob

1. Walking is ___Molly___'s favourite hobby.   >   She wants to go for a walk.

2. The weather is cold and wet.   >   _____ doesn't want to go out.

3. _____ doesn't want to go for a walk.   >   She's very tired today.

4. _____ wants to see the waterfall.   >   He wants to go for a walk.

5. The mountains are beautiful.   >   _____ would like to walk in the mountains.

6. _____ wouldn't like to come for a walk.   >   He doesn't like walking.

Join the sentences with so.

Walking is Molly's favourite hobby, so she wants to go for a walk.

Now join the sentences with because.

Molly wants to go for a walk because walking is her favourite hobby.

Teacher/parent note : These activities consolidate *so* and *because*. Pupils listen and fill in the names to complete the sentences. They then join these sentences using *so* and *because* to express reason.

Writing page 80

 # Reading

Read. Tick (✓) or cross (✗).

Sue isn't hot. She's got a bottle of cold water.

May is hot. She's angry.

Max is under a tree. He isn't hot. He isn't happy. He hasn't got any bananas.

Bill is happy. He doesn't have to go to school. He's very tired. He's sleeping.

Pex likes swimming. He's afraid. He can see a fish in the water.

Sam is hungry. He wants an ice-cream. He can't buy one. He hasn't got any money.

1. Sam can't buy an ice-cream. ____✓____

2. Max wants a banana. _____

3. Sue wants a bottle of cold water. _____

4. Pex is afraid of the water. _____

5. May is enjoying her game of tennis. _____

6. Bill isn't enjoying his trip to the beach. _____

Make sentences. Use but, so or because.

Sue isn't hot because she's got a bottle of cold water.

Let's practise!

but ...   so ...   because ...

Teacher/parent note : These activities consolidate the conjunctions encountered so far. Pupils read about a trip to the beach and decide if statements about the text are true or false. They then connect the short sentences with *but, so* and *because* to make long sentences.

Revision Unit 2

 Listening

What do they like doing? When do they do these things? Listen and draw lines.

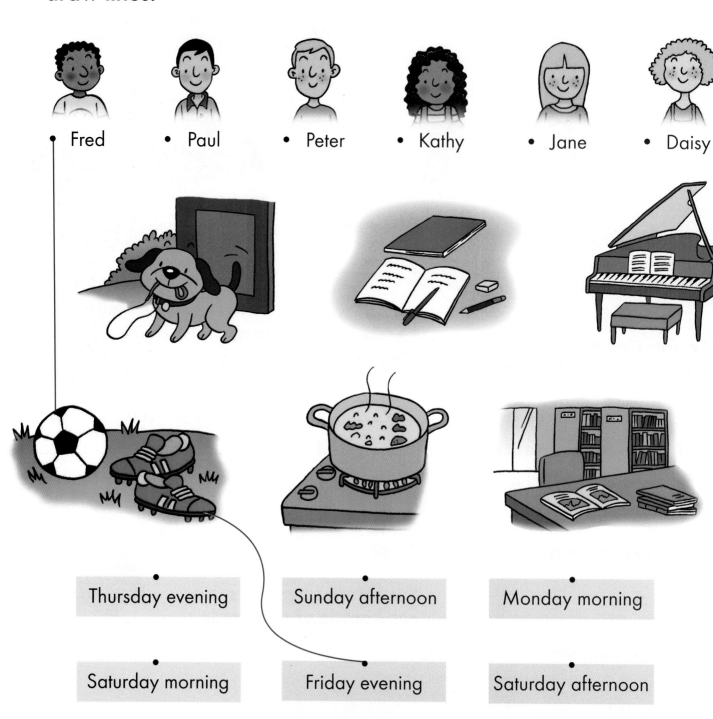

Fred • Paul • Peter • Kathy • Jane • Daisy

Thursday evening • Sunday afternoon • Monday morning

Saturday morning • Friday evening • Saturday afternoon

Teacher/parent note : In this activity, pupils practise listening for *likes doing* and the days of the week. They listen and draw lines to match the children to the activities they like doing, and when they like doing them.

Reading

Look at the robots. Read and write the letters.

1. __f__   2. ____   3. ____   4. ____   5. ____   6. ____

a. I'm stronger than all the robots here.

b. I'm taller than one robot next to me but I'm shorter than the other.

c. Can you help me, please? I'm the weakest robot here.

d. I'm the cleanest robot here. Mr Lee cleans me every day.

e. My computer can do a lot of things. I'm the cleverest robot here!

f. I'm the dirtiest robot here! Mr Lee's got to clean me.

Teacher/parent note : In this activity, pupils revise comparative and superlative adjectives. They match the correct sentences with the robots in the picture.

Speaking

Talk about the food.

What food and drinks are there?

There is a plate of chicken and potatoes. There is a bottle of lemonade.

Now ask and answer. Use the words in the box to help you.

| breakfast | lunch | dinner |

 What would you like for breakfast today?

I'd like a box of sandwiches, please.

Teacher/parent note : The first activity revises vocabulary for containers, food and drinks. In the second activity, pupils practise saying what they would like to have for breakfast and lunch.

Reading

Read and write the words.

1. This is made of two pieces of bread with some
   meat and vegetables between them.

   _____a sandwich_____

2. This is a very small town.

   _____

3. Fish live here but it's not a river. It's not the sea too.

   _____

4. This is round. Cars have four of these.

   _____

5. Pupils have to do this after school.

   _____

6. You can have this at the beach, at a waterfall
   or at the park. There are food and drinks.

   _____

7. You can find a lot of trees here.

   _____

8. You put food on this when you eat.

   _____

Teacher/parent note : This activity revises vocabulary introduced in this book. Pupils read the clues and write the words.

Word List

Animals
kangaroo	10
bat	18
whale	33

Countries and nationalities
Australia	7
Australian	6
Canada	33
China	7
Chinese	6
England	7
English	6
India	7
Indian	6
Malaysia	7
Malaysian	6
Thai	6
Thailand	7

Food and drink
coffee	10
salad	69
soup	63
tea	26

The body and face
beard	12
blonde	12
curly	12
fair	12
fat	13
moustache	12
neck	12
shoulder	12
tall	13
thin	13

Words that tell about time
after	21
always	19
before	21
early	79
every day	62
Friday	58
Monday	58
never	19
often	19
on	58
once	62
past	36
Saturday	58
sometimes	19
Sunday	58
Thursday	58
time	60
Tuesday	58
twice	62
Wednesday	58
week	62
weekend	70

Places
bank	38
building	40
bus station	38
café	38
cinema	38
farm	76
ground floor	40
hospital	38
library	38
lift	40
market	26
place	39
shop	37
supermarket	39
swimming pool	39

At home
basement	40
sitting room	27
shelf	67

Family, friends and ourselves
age	11
Annie	6
Chung	7
Daisy	42
Fred	42
grandparents	60
Jack	12
Jane	42
John	6
Kathy	42
Lek	7
Mack	12
Paul	42
Peter	40
Salina	7
Sunita	6
Zack	12

People
pirate	12

Ordinal numbers
first	36
second	36
third	36
fourth	36
fifth	36
sixth	36
seventh	36

eighth	37	sailing	70	free	60
ninth	37	shopping	70	go shopping	38
tenth	37	skating	70	hungry	53
		wheel	46	last	38

The world around us

forest	32
lake	52
mountain	32
nest	37
river	32
sky	31
town	52
village	76
waterfall	64

Containers

bin	24
bottle	64
bowl	64
cup	26
plate	64

School and classrooms

email	41
homework	60
list	25
map	53
race	48
rubbish	24
tests	27

Sports and play

cage	20
diary	60
holiday	32
invitation	61
menu	69
picnic	64

The weather

blow	30
cloudy	31
cold	31
hot	30
rain	31
shine	30
snow	30
weather	31
wet	30
windy	30

Clothes

coat	13
scarf	13
sweater	34

Words that tell more about people/things (adjectives)

a lot	18
afraid	46
all	38
angry	54
awake	21
best	52
better	50
bottom	76
clever	72
different	48
difficult	72
empty	24
false	35
fair	13

free	60
go shopping	38
hungry	53
last	38
loud	50
much	73
over	49
pleased	8
quick	48
right	20
round	46
silly	72
sleepy	10
slow	48
square	46
straight	12
strong	46
thirsty	53
tidy	24
tired	46
true	35
unusual	72
worse	51
worst	54
wrong	64

Action words (verbs)

be called	13
bring	72
brush	24
buy	26
circle	33
clean	22
come (from)	7
complete	78
get (up)	21
guess	35
hate	74
hear	9

Now I know **231** more words! Wow!